Executive Presence-Improv Style!

Lisa Safran, MA

Executive Presence- Improv Style!

*A Guide to Improvising
Your Way into Executive Presence!*

Lisa Safran, MA

ISBN: 978-0-9857818-0-4

Published by:

Princess Ellen Publishing

www.improvconsultants.com

415-484-5871

info@improvconsultants.com

Dedication

This book is dedicated to all of you who are willing to boldly say "YES, AND" in order to move your life or business forward.

Table of Contents

Table Of Contents..I

Preface: A Leadership Journey II

Acknowledgments VI

Introduction: Executive Presence- Improv Style! VIII

How To Use This Book.. XIV

The Tenets Of Improvisation 2

Executive Presence Self- Assessment................................4

Scoring Guide... 6

Executive Presence Exercises 7

Internal Presence Exercises 8

Professional Presence Exercises..................................... 21

Leadership Presence Exercises 35

Moving The Story Forward Exercises............................ 48

Sample Improv Menu.. 64

Activity Index... 65

About The Author... 67

Preface: A Leadership Journey

"RUUUUN!" The word echoed against the empty sea, as boats smashed into a million pieces. Silence replaced by a cacophony of terror. I took off chased by an unseen monster. As I ran inland from the beach, people ran toward me, some covered with blood, but all covered with fear. I took shelter in a gazebo wondering which way to go. A terrible cracking sound erupted and a chef bedecked by a tall white hat came kicking through a bamboo fence, followed by a frightened Thai women wearing long silk dresses and flip flops, and a tourist dressed in white carrying a wicker basket. The chef ran by me and began scrambling up the hill and like the white rabbit in <u>Alice in Wonderland</u>, we all followed. I watched the tall white hat bob between the dark green vines and trees and desperately tried to keep it in sight. This hat felt like my salvation.

Several hours later at an evacuation area I reunited with my traveling companion. Together with newfound friends, we got through the night. Thai women collected fish from the beach and made curry that kicked my heart and soul into life. We watched the news and slept little that night. In the morning, along with hundreds of tourists and locals, we boarded boats piled high with belongings to make our way to Krabi, 45 minutes away. I stood on the deck looking out at the debris of homes, luggage, and trees floating by on the water. Except for a young Thai girl whispering unknown words to her pet bunny that she clutched to her chest, the rest of us were silent.

Here is what I know.

On the morning of December 26th, 2004 I was an elementary school teacher on vacation in Thailand. I was a former actress, stand up comic, and musician — all of which I missed terribly (except being a stand up comic...I just wasn't that funny). I had thrown it all out to lead a "responsible life," that was secure. By afternoon, I had survived one of the deadliest natural disasters in our century and was consumed with survivor's guilt and felt anything but secure.

From this place of despair and regret I looked at my life and from the silence came sound— The sound of creativity, the sound of passion, the sound of strength. There is an improvisation game called "New Choice" where a director will either call out "new choice" or rings a bell, letting the improviser know that they need to change what they last said. Sometimes the bell will keep ringing until the director feels satisfied. The bell had rung, and it was loud.

There were three items on my list of things I must do to live a fuller life.

Create a business that truly blended my creativity with my education

Produce an album of my original music

Live overseas

The first two seemed impossible, but living overseas as a teacher was completely doable. In August of 2005, I boarded a plane to Bangkok.

I taught a 3rd grade class with students mainly from the Mekong region and several from other parts of the world. I used improvisational theatre games to support teaching language arts and quickly noticed that students not only enjoyed the games, but developed increased confidence in speaking and presenting. Picking up a cheap guitar I began to compose music- feeling my way around the strings and listening for sounds that would break the silence.

Two years came and went and a cold foggy San Francisco summer day welcomed me home in 2007.

Then there were two things on my list.

Create a business that truly blended my creativity with my education

Produce an album of my original music

Upon returning home I developed a program on using improvisation to build literacy and began writing a book. In 2010 <u>Reading and Writing Come Alive: Using Improvisation to Build Literacy</u> was published and I presented workshops on the topic at various conferences around the country. That same year I produced *Dreams that Matter,* a CD of original music, some of which were songs composed on my cheap guitar sitting on the balcony overlooking the Gulf of Thailand.

And then there was one thing left on my list.

Create a business that truly blended my creativity with my education

There is something about starting a business that feels a bit like standing on the edge of a cliff and knowing that the only way off of it is to jump but all you see is a raging river below with sharp protruding rocks. I jumped anyway.

It's been two years since filing my DBA as Improv Consultants. I still sometimes feel like I am on the edge of a cliff but the passion and joy this work brings to me and others provides a soft landing each time, I am willing to take the risk. Improvisation is all about saying yes to the offer and moving the story forward. I thought the *story* of my new business was that I would provide staff development to teachers around the area of literacy. Then a tech firm in San Francisco asked me to facilitate an improvisational business training to support team building. I said, Yes…and then an individual asked me to help them develop confidence to lead more effective presentations and I said, YES again. Individuals wanting to free themselves from the perceived constraints of standing on various cliffs looking down only able to see raging water and rugged rocks also sought me out- and I helped them see the brilliance of the sky, the joy of the water splashing, and that anything is possible when you move the story forward.

There was a new thing on my list.

Create a new list and continue the story!

Acknowledgments

I'd like to acknowledge my inspiring clients who bring out creativity and foster engagement among the people they lead and who inspire me to continue to learn and grow. To my wonderful parents- Dad, Mom, and Naomi! My sister, Misha and my brother, Adam- my wonderful step siblings Tamar, Shanti, and Aaron. To my friends who meet each Thursday at noon and Susan (my voice of reason) and to Ami and our ongoing affirmation lists supporting vision and change. To Sue Walden, Kenn Adams, Caterina Rando and Rebecca Stockley for being exceptionally creative and talented! To all my improv teachers past and present who taught me many of the activities included in this book. Also to my friend and colleague Craig Harrison for his support and seeing the sweet and crunchy in *"peanut-peanut butter."*

"We keep moving forward, opening new doors, and doing new things, because we're curious and curiosity keeps leading us down new paths."

—Walt Disney

Introduction: Executive Presence- Improv Style!

When I first launched my business, Improv Consultants in 2011 I had a specific idea of what it would entail. I was going to provide staff development for teachers around the area of literacy development. With 12 years of teaching experience, this seemed like an effortless transition. When I was asked to lead a staff development for a tech firm in SF to support team building and communication- while somewhat nervous as this was slightly out of my comfort zone- this also seemed plausible and in line with my expertise. One of the tenets in improv is to risk failure- what did I really have to lose? I jumped in, facilitated the training, and was excited to be invited back to do a subsequent training with the rest of the team.

Another rule of improv is to say, "Yes...and." This rule suggests that when presented with an offer, we accept the offer and add something to move the story forward. Saying yes to leading the tech firm staff development, even though nervous, is a concrete example of applying that rule- Jumping in, even if it meant not doing it perfectly is an example of "risking failure," something that is very scary for most people to do in today's society. However if we think about some of the visionaries who have risked failure in their work, we might think Ghandi, the Wright Brothers, or Steve Jobs.

Within 3 months of filing my business name, I received a contract to deliver a 3-day training at the Green School in Bali. While there, an expat business woman from the community approached me and asked if I worked with individuals. My first thought was, "What? Improv for one? How would that work?" Thankfully I kept my thoughts to myself and replied "Sure, what did you have in mind?" Little did I know that this willingness to say yes would be the beginning of my executive coaching practice. Just as when performing during an improvisation show, an improviser often only has a small idea, if that, of where to start. Perhaps it's something physical, an emotion, or a character. Perhaps it is just the willingness to walk onto the stage and do nothing. Improvisers trust the other players to support and step in when needed. They do this by accepting the offer that was given and moving the story forward. My role as an executive presence coach started with the request of the Bali business woman asking for help. I said yes and asked for more information to guide me in supporting her. I spent the next few days preparing for our session by researching best coaching practices, reviewing improvisation activities that would support her specific goals, and creating an agenda for our session. After our 2 hour appointment was over, while elated and energized by the experience, I saw it only as a fluke, one time experience and something that would soon be just one more memory from my experience in Bali.

Upon returning to San Francisco I began the journey of actively marketing and networking for my business. I attended networking events and took a class in using public speaking to leverage your business by Coach Caterina Rando (http://caterinarando.com). I heard Caterina speak at a dinner of the National Association of

Women Business Owners (http://www.nawbo.org) and was impressed with her genuineness and practical approach. She was offering a 2-day *Sought After Speaker Summit* and my new acquaintance at the table I was seated at invited me to attend as her guest, in exchange for providing her with an individual coaching session. This would be coaching session #2. She was seeking some clarity around a business idea. I thought about her goals, researched various coaching methods and again brought in various improvisation exercises to support meeting those goals. By the end of our hour together she had a clearer idea of her business and a tag line to go with it.

In October 2011 I joined BNI (http://bni.com), an international referral networking association. Attending a weekly meeting at 7AM began to teach me how to further show up for my business- one that was not very clearly defined but certainly had passion! I was an improv consultant- what was that? I was a trainer. How did improv and business training fit together? I also led staff trainings for teachers. I had written a guide book for teachers in 2010, <u>Reading and Writing Come Alive: Using Improvisation to Build Literacy</u>. I was funny and thought on my feet and could teach you to do the same. Oh, and did I mention that I also provide party entertainment? It was a wonder I received any referrals at all with all the confusion. In improvisation we speak about daring to be dull or obvious and to not give so many offers that a story line is impossible to find. I was a walking example of why this can be a problem. Having so many ways to apply improv was too confusing to most people. Regardless, I struggled along and continued to work part time while finding my voice as a business owner.

In January 2012, I moved to Marin County resulting in transferring to a new BNI chapter. During the switch, it was suggested by the membership committee that I say I was an *Improv Consultant specializing in training programs for businesses, schools, and individuals.* Somehow this seemed clearer and I resonated with it in a way that helped me achieve more focus. Now meeting on Friday mornings, my 30 second pitch became slightly clearer, although it could still stand to be refined and improved. My 7 minute presentations were an opportunity to facilitate improvisation, employ various presentation strategies, engage my audience, and shine! People began to ask me for help in developing their presentation skills. Improving my online presence, I began to receive requests from clients out of the area and even out of state to coach them on developing and delivering solid presentations. My dream of combining my love of performance with education was being realized. This was fun!

So how did this improv consultant become an executive presence coach? Another aspect of improvisation is that during a scene an improviser might endow a fellow actor with certain qualities or characteristics. The other actor then accepts those endowments as they offer a wonderful opportunity to enhance their character or some aspect of the story they are creating. I was endowed with being an Executive Presence Coach during the BNI annual holiday party. One of my BNI colleagues was speaking to my date about a possible client who needed executive presence coaching. My date was a speaker and a trainer. My BNI colleague was offering that referral to my date to which he laughed and replied, "While I certainly appreciate the referral, you have an Executive Presence Coach in your group- Lisa." They both started laughing. This is when I entered the scene and asked what was so funny. My BNI colleague related the tale and asked me if this is what I was. I had never even heard the phrase before and had no idea. I asked what it was and how I fit the bill. The following questions were asked:

1.   Do you help people gain confidence in their communication?

2.   Do you support people in finding passion in what they do?

3.   Do you teach presentation strategies for engaging audiences?

4.   Do you help people develop courage to take risks?

The answers to all these questions were Yes...*and* I help them to develop humor and spontaneity.

Thus, an Executive Presence Coach was born.

There are many wonderful resources and books available that will support a deeper understanding of Executive Presence. In short, Executive Presence is the ability to communicate, motivate, inspire, and influence outcomes.

It is also characterized by the ability to be present and give undivided attention, to speak honestly from the heart and in a unique manner. Strong leaders know how to command a room with presence.

Each person striving to increase or develop Executive Presence needs to develop his or her own authentic way or brand. Someone with presence might be magnetic or charismatic but equally could be someone quiet and contemplative; these qualities might be interchangeable depending on the situation. It all depends on the unique character of the individual. This is good news. It means that <u>anyone</u> is capable of strengthening and developing their Executive Presence. The exercises in this book will help you begin to do just that!

To learn more about executive presence, I highly recommend the following two resources:

<u>The Three Levels of Leadership</u> by James Scouller

<u>Leadership Presence</u> by Belle Linda Halpern and Kathy Lubar

How to Use This Book

"To try is to risk failure. But risk must be taken because the greatest hazard of life is to risk nothing. The person who risks nothing does nothing, has nothing, is nothing. He may avoid suffering and sorrow, but he simply cannot learn, feel, change, grow, live, and love."

—Leo Buscaglia

The aim of this book is to help you increase your confidence and strengthen your executive presence. The exercises included in this book are ones that I continue to practice and use with my coaching clients. They are divided into the following categories:

- Internal Presence Exercises

- Professional Presence Exercises

- Leadership Presence Exercises

- Moving the Story Forward Exercises

The *Internal Presence* exercises support relaxation, focus, and clarity. They will support building a practice to develop a clear vision of how you'd like to see yourself, your day, your career, your life, and the interactions you have with others.

The *Professional Presence* section includes exercises to

support vocal tone, delivery, and body awareness exercises.

The *Leadership Presence* section supports building capacity for risk taking, being spontaneous, and being bold.

The *Moving the Story Forward* section includes activities to support creating an action plan, various strategies for setting goals, and following through.

The exercises in this book integrate various improvisation, coaching, and even relaxation methods, moving between breathing exercises, physical activities, writing assignments, art projects, and suggested actions to take to develop or strengthen your executive presence. It is truly a hands on experience and the only way to create change is to practice the exercises regularly.

Supply List
Journal/Notebook
Drawing paper or poster board
Drawing markers
Highlighters
Popsicle Sticks
Permanent Marker
Magazines and/or other resources for pictures and images
Scissors
Glue
Timer (if you use your phone, I recommend putting it in airplane mode so that you will not be disturbed.)

I suggest that you get a special notebook or journal that you dedicate specifically for this work.

Start by reviewing the *Tenets of Improvisation*. Consider how these tenets apply currently in your life. Copy the tenets into your journal or notebook and write about each one. Which tenets are you already adhering to and in what ways? Which ones seem challenging and why?

Next, set a timer for 2 minutes and complete the *Executive Presence Self-Assessment*. Make a copy of the assessment to retake along the way in order to observe areas of growth and improvement. Review the *Scoring Guide*. What did you notice? Are there any patterns?

Schedule regular times each week to dedicate to the exercises in this book.

Some of the exercises included are best with 2 or more people. Find a business partner, friend, or experienced coach to practice the exercises with you. Whenever possible, I will explain how you can do the exercise solo.

At the beginning of each session with a client, I always start by asking the following questions:

- What were some successes over the past week?

- What were some challenges over the past week?

- What would you like to work on today?

To get the most out of this book, keep a journal and plan on starting each practice session by asking and answering those questions in writing.

When I work with clients, I use the information given to guide our session, selecting specific exercises that will address the current needs. For example, if when answering the question about challenges, the topic of listening or connecting with others during a conversation was a challenge, focus your practice session on those exercises that enhance listening skills. If the areas of challenge are around goal setting or follow through, revisit the *Internal Presence and Moving the Story Forward* exercises. See the *Sample Improv Menu* for some ideas on how to put a self directed agenda together.

After completing each exercise answer the following questions in your journal or notebook.

- How did that feel?

- What actually happened?

- What did you learn?

- What did you learn to be more successful?

- What would happen if you did this daily?

- How will you use or apply this?

That's pretty much it! Enjoy and remember to find the joy in failure.*

*Thank you to Rebecca Stockley for the debriefing questions

"Be brave enough to live life creatively. The creative is the place where no one else has ever been. You have to leave the city of your comfort and go into the wilderness of your intuition. You can't get there by bus, only by hard work and risk and by not quite knowing what you are doing. What you'll discover will be wonderful. What you'll discover will be yourself."

—Alan Alda

The Tenets of Improvisation

Say Yes and <u>add positively</u> to the situation
Fully accept ideas, offers and add a new piece of information to serve the bigger picture. This does not mean that we have to agree with each other all the time. In fact, the most successful teams have a healthy amount of disagreement and debate. But listening and taking in all aspects of an idea before negating, supports building relationships and creating healthy respect.

Stay present—evaluate later
Staying present to each moment and refraining from planning allows for even more options and choices to make themselves known.

Make your partner look brilliant
This eliminates defensiveness. The partner can literally be a partner, or it could be a colleague, subordinate, or even the company itself.

Look for connection
Finding commonalities with others supports the building of healthy relationships. Where do you agree?

Allow yourself to be changed
By staying in the moment, we are more likely to be able to take in new information which can be an invitation to make a new choice, inspire new ideas, and make changes.

Serve the bigger picture

When performing, we refer to this rule as serving the platform (story or scene). In other words, the actor makes choices to support the story as opposed to only serving his or her own need to do something special. What is the bigger picture in your life? What is the bigger picture to support the business or team?

Find the joy in failure: Be willing to make mistakes

One of the key components great leaders have is the willingness to risk failure. They put themselves on the line for their vision and ideas. Be willing to make mistakes and find the joy in failure. See each mistake, not so much as a failure but the willingness to be courageous.

Executive Presence Self- Assessment

Rate the following statements by scoring each statement 1-4. 4- being always, 3- sometimes, 2- rarely, 1- never. Write down the first number that comes to mind as quickly as possible. Apply the question to where you are in your life right now. Some of the questions refer to colleagues or a team- adapt that to friends or business relations if you are not presently working with a team or staff. Set a timer for 2 minutes to support moving through this swiftly.

		Score 1-4
1	I am a creative thinker.	
2	I am able to speak clearly to others.	
3	I am comfortable making mistakes.	
4	I am comfortable trying new things.	
5	I am courageous.	
6	I am flexible.	
7	I am good at solving problems.	
8	I can inspire others into action.	
9	I develop and implement action plans that support the overall vision.	
10	I encourage others to dream and think big.	
11	I enjoy delivering presentations.	

12	I feel comfortable answering questions that I haven't prepared for.	
13	I feel comfortable thinking on the spot.	
14	I feel confident as a leader.	
15	I listen carefully when others are speaking.	
16	I possess a positive attitude toward change.	
17	I see the overall big picture.	
18	I view problems as opportunities.	
19	Colleagues/staff feel safe speaking their mind around me.	
20	Colleagues/staff know that they can offer alternate opinions	
21	I am confident speaking/presenting to a small group.	
22	I am confident speaking/presenting to a large group.	
23	I feel comfortable improvising.	
24	My colleagues/staff feels respected by me.	
25	My colleagues/staff feel comfortable coming to me with new ideas.	

Scoring Guide

Score the survey by adding up the numbers: _____

A score of eighty-five to one hundred indicates very strong Executive Presence. The next step is to continue to develop presence and the ability to effectively inspire teams through including various engagement strategies. Pay attention to the items where a score of 1-3 were noted and focus on strengthening those specific areas. Additionally, a high score could mean that you are ready for a more challenging position or goal. Consider setting a new course and creating new goals.

A score of seventy to eighty-four indicates strong Executive Presence. Continue to work on those areas where a score of 1-3 were evident.

A score of seventy or less indicates potential discomfort when it comes to presentation skills, effective leadership or responding to change. Practicing the activities in this book will support strengthening your executive presence and leadership skills. Consider hiring a coach to support you throughout the process.

No matter what the score is, a commitment, desire, and determination toward professional growth are the biggest indicators of ability to becoming an effective leader who possesses executive presence.

Executive Presence Exercises

Illustration by Rich Sigberman

"I start with the premise that the function of leadership is to produce more leaders, not more followers."

—Ralph Nader

Please consult a physician before doing any of the physical or vocal exercises listed in this book.

Internal Presence Exercises

Exercises in this Section:

1. Vertebrae Roll Up and Down
2. Breathing
3. Breathing and Vocalizing
4. Counting 1-8
5. Who Are You?
6. Who Am I?
7. 60 Second Life
8. Visualization
9. What Do You See?
10. Ideal Day
11. Pros and Cons
12. Vision Board

"The more of me I be, the clearer I can see."

—Rachel Andrews

Exercise Title: Vertebrae Roll Up and Down

Exercise Purpose: To relax and become present

Instructions:

Stand straight with your feet hips width apart, and your head and neck in a comfortable position. Imagine you are a tree and that your feet are firmly rooted in the ground. While taking deep breaths into your diaphragm, slowly start to roll your spine down toward the floor. Start with your head and neck, and slowly work down your spine rolling each vertebrae one at a time releasing & letting go. Visualize your spine as a string of pearls. Stop at areas of tightness, stiffness, or lack of movement. Roll up and down through these areas until the tissue warms up allowing you to roll further.

Allow the weight of your head to gently pull your spine all the way down until you end up with your head, neck, torso and arms dangling toward your feet. Feel free to bend your knees as you bend over to release any tension in your back. Make sure your neck is relaxed.

Allow your arms to sway back and forth. Breathe in and out and upon exhale, allow a sound to escape.

Roll back up reversing the process. You will end upright with your head, neck, torso, arms and lower extremities relaxed.

Spend from 5-10 minutes doing this exercise.

Exercise Title: Breathing

Exercise Purpose: To relax and become present

Instructions:

Sit comfortably with eyes closed, being present without thinking or judging. Notice sounds, physical sensations, thoughts, and feelings. Do this without trying to fix or change it. Just be. Do this until you feel yourself settling down.

Take several breaths in through your nose and audibly exhale through your mouth. With each exhale, allow any tension you feel to exit the body.

Begin to breath in and out through the nose quietly and in a relaxed manner. Notice where your mind drifts to without judgment.

A quick body scan starting from the top of your head will help you notice where you might be carrying tension, discomfort, and where your body feels good. Do not spend much time on this and there's no need to try to fix or change anything. Just be aware of where you are at.

Count your breaths- inhale- 1, exhale 2. Count up to 10 and then start again at 1. If you lose track just start over. Allow all of your experiences — thoughts, emotions, bodily sensations, to come and go in the background and focus on each breath.

Now allow yourself to stop counting your breaths and to let your mind run free. Where does it go? What does it focus on?

Again, return to counting each breath. Then stop and focus again on the sounds around you. Bring your awareness to your body and how it feels in the chair. When you are ready, open your eyes.

Start with 3 minutes and extend this practice to 30 or more each day.

Exercise Title: Breathing and Vocalizing

Exercise Purpose: To relax the voice

Instructions:

Lie on your back with your knees in the air and your eyes closed. Become aware of how your body feels as your breathe in and out naturally. As you notice, release the tension by breathing into that area of your body (this is done by visualizing the area and then imagining yourself breathing out the tension or pain). The goal of the exercise is to relax all areas of your body that affect your voice. Important areas to focus on include the jaw, neck, shoulders, chest, upper and lower back, and diaphragm. Breathe in deeply to expand your lung capacity.

As your body relaxes, prop your head back slightly and release your jaw so that it gapes open. There should be no tension in your neck, chest, shoulders or jaw. Take in a deep breath, and as you breathe out, vocalize. It will sound like an open-mouthed moan. As you vocalize, pay close attention to your jaw, neck, shoulders, back and chest. Most likely, they will tense up when you vocalize. Keep practicing until you can vocalize without tensing your muscles.[1]

---

[1] Adapted from: http://www.wikihow.com/Develop-a-Perfect-Speaking-Voice

Exercise Title: Counting 1-8

Exercise Purpose: To relax, warm up, and allow yourself to play big!

Instructions:

Standing upright, shake right hand…counting loudly, "1-2-3-4-5-6-7-8." Then shake left hand… counting "1-2-3-4-5-6-7-8." Next, shake right foot, again counting "1-2-3-4-5-6-7-8", and then shake left foot counting "1-2-3-4-5-6-7-8."

Start over and repeat the steps, counting "1-2-3-4-5-6-7" this round.

Next, continue to start a new round, repeating each step and counting loudly, dropping the count by 1 until the final round will be '1'. For the final round, put arms above head spread eagle and legs apart yelling, "Wooo-Hoo!"

Exercise Title:	Who Are You?
Exercise Purpose:	To gain focus and clarity while thinking outside the box

Instructions:

Set a timer for 1-3 minutes (1 minute to begin with and then gradually stretch yourself to go longer each time).

With two people, one person keeps asking the other the question, "Who are you?" and the second person responds with a short answer. *I am a woman. I am a bird. I am happiness.*

Alternatively, the exercise can be played where one person asks the question and the partner answers, and then the partner asks the question and the first person answers—going back and forth rapidly until the time is complete.

Upon completing the timed portion of the exercise, take a few minutes to write down some of the responses you gave. Noting any surprising answers or patterns that may have emerged.

Solo:

Set a timer for 1-3 minutes. Write the question: Who Are You? in the header of a piece of paper or in your journal. Write the answer to the question as many times in as many different ways as possible before the time runs out.

Exercise Title: Who Am I?

Exercise Purpose: To gain focus clarity, and empathy
while thinking outside the box

Instructions:

Set a timer for 1-3 minutes (1 minute to begin with and then gradually stretch yourself to go longer each time).

Think about someone you are having challenges with. Take some time to visualize them and the interactions you have had.

Set a timer for 1-3 minutes. Write the question: Who Am I? in the header of a piece of paper or in your journal. Imagine yourself as this person and write the answer to the question as many times and in as many different ways as possible before the time runs out.

Review your answers and look for commonalities and answers that increase feelings of empathy. Notice how your interaction is with the person the next time you see him or her. Did it change? Did you change?

| **Exercise Title:** | 60 Second Life |
| **Exercise Purpose:** | To gain clarity on where you have been and where you might want to go |

Instructions:

Set a timer for 1 minute. This activity is best played in pairs.

For 60 seconds one partner, tells anything they want about their life in 60 seconds while the other partner listens (doesn't interject, comment, or question). Then the listening partner, retells what they heard. The "telling" partner only listens to what was heard without commenting, correcting, or interjecting. Then the process is reversed. After both partners have completed the cycle, debrief the process by asking yourselves the following questions:

- How did that feel?

- What actually happened as we did that?

- What did you tend to focus on during your 60 seconds? Facts? Feelings? Events?

- What did you learn?

- What would happen if you had only 30 seconds (or 90 seconds)?

- How might you use or apply this activity?

Solo:

Set a timer for 1 minute. Write about your life for 1 minute as fast as you can- stream of consciousness. Upon completing the exercise, respond to the debrief questions above by writing down your responses.

Exercise Title: Visualization

Exercise Purpose: To gain clarity, build confidence, and
                        reduce stress

Instructions:

Begin by doing the breathing exercise to support relaxation.

This exercise is best performed with a partner who can guide you through the visualization.

When guiding my clients, I use important information they have shared with me to create the visualization. For example, when preparing for a presentation, I will guide the client in seeing themselves confidently get ready for the presentation the night before. Then reinforce the good night sleep they had and move into preparing for leaving the house, knowing that everything is prepared and ready to go. Upon arriving at the location, I remind the client that they have practiced and prepared sufficiently and have the expertise to deliver an outstanding presentation. The idea of a visualization is to imagine your success and completing the task with ease. To do this independently, write out your vision of the best case scenario and then take yourself through each step during the relaxation exercise.

Solo:

Pre-record a visualization that will support you in preparing for your event, meeting, or presentation. Use the recording to guide you through the exercise.

Exercise Title: What Do You See?

Exercise Purpose: To improve focus and being present

Instructions:

Begin by doing the breathing exercise. Upon completion, look around the room you are in. Then close your eyes. What do you see? What do you remember? See how many details you can remember and then open your eyes. What was accurate? What was not? What did you not see or remember at all? Why do we remember some things and not others?

This can be practiced out in public where there are people to observe. Look at someone for about 15-30 seconds and then close your eyes.

- What do you remember?
- What color hair did the person have? Eyes?
- What type of outfit? Shoes?
- What was the fabric?
- What was the expression on their face?
- What length were their eye lashes?
- How thick were their eyebrows?
- How tall were they in relation to you?

Exercise Title: Ideal Day

Exercise Purpose: To support focus and goal setting

Instructions:

Begin by doing the breathing exercise. Once relaxed, think about your typical day. What do you usually do from the time you wake up to when you retire at night? If you could create your ideal schedule what would it look like? Would you start by checking email or would you take a lovely walk instead?

Take some time to write out your current schedule. For each entry assign it a category. Categories could include:

- Self Care
- Personal Maintenance
- Business Development
- Friends/Family
- Dating
- Exercise
- Health
- Bill Paying
- Travel Time

Review the completed chart. How balanced is your current schedule? What would it take to create more balance?

Exercise Title: Pros and Cons

Exercise Purpose: To support focus and goal setting

Instructions:

Begin by doing the breathing exercise. Once relaxed, think about your current job or business. What do you love about it? What gives you passion? What about it motivates you to show up each day for it? What do you find stressful? Are you unhappy? Do you want a change?

Take some time to write out the pros and cons of your current position. Take note of the amount of positive versus negative entries. For each entry, score it 1-10 points (10 being very important). Example:

Pros		Cons	
I set my own schedule	8	I work a lot of hours to make ends meet	5
I am excited about the quality of the work I do	10	There is a lot to do being self-employed and it all falls on me	8
My work is super creative!	10	Sometimes the work is isolating	5
I am doing what I love!	10	Business development is challenging	10
Total	38	Total	28

So while there were equal pros and cons, the pros earned more points making the qualities of the current position still more desirable than perhaps changing direction at this point.

Exercise Title: Vision Board

Exercise Purpose: To create a graphic representation of what you truly want

Instructions:

Give yourself 30-45 minutes, in a quiet space. With all your materials around you – set the intention that you are going to create a vision for yourself and set a timeline- for example: this vision will materialize in 6 months or 1 year.

Consider using one or more of the following questions to reflect upon before starting your vision board.

Questions:

- If you had no fear, what would you do?

- What does your perfect day look & feel like? (what do you do in the morning, afternoon, evening)?

- How are you helping others?

Supply List
• Drawing paper or poster board
• Drawing markers
• Magazines and/or other resources for pictures and images
• Scissors
• Glue

Flip thru the magazines and rip out images and words that jump out at you and with which you have an emotional connection with, piling them off to the side. Do this for about 15 minutes.

Assemble the images and words you have ripped out onto your drawing paper or poster board. There is no wrong way to do this. Follow your intuition and do what feels right for you. Play around with the images for a while until you feel they are in the right place. Then glue them. Place the board somewhere where you can enjoy and reflect upon it daily.

Professional Presence Exercises

Exercises in this Section:

1. Vocal Tones

2. Tongue Twisters

3. Enunciation

4. Mirror

5. What Changed?

6. Body Language

7. Does the Story Serve You? Part 1

8. Does the Story Serve You? Part 2

9. Voice Mirror

10. Faster Slower

11. Best Worst

12. Character Voices

13. Super Man/Woman Poses

"They may forget what you said, but they will never forget how you made them feel."

—Carl W. Buechner

Exercise Title: Vocal Tones

Exercise Purpose: To broaden range and presence using voice

Instructions:

1ˢᵗ Exercise:

Hum at a comfortable pitch. Next, move the pitch slightly lower. Be aware of how the sound vibrates and feels in your chest. Keep humming until you feel the vibration in your chest and then increase the intensity of the vibration. Next, move the hum into a higher register until you feel it in your head. Let your mouth open. Keep humming and become aware of where the vibration is. Finally, return the pitch to your chest and repeat. Always end in the chest hum with full vibration.

2ⁿᵈ Exercise:

Start by standing straight, feet shoulder width apart, shoulders relaxed. Take a nice deep breath into your diaphragm and open your mouth. Focusing on the top back of your mouth, allow a sigh with the sound, "aaaahhh" to roll out as if it is a siren. Imagine that the sound starts at the top of your head and moves down all the way to your toes. The sound should be smooth and effortless. Once it is a low sound, take another breath into your diaphragm and then roll the sound from your toes all the way back up to your head.

Exercise Title: Tongue Twisters

Exercise Purpose: To strengthen articulation

Instructions:

Articulation: Find a tongue twister to practice. There are plenty available on the internet. Start by reading it slowly. Allow your tongue and lips to carefully form each word as your read the tongue twister in its entirety. Next read it as fast as you can. When you are able to read it super fast with zero mistakes, find a new tongue twister and start again.

Peter Piper picked a peck of pickled peppers.

A peck of pickled peppers Peter Piper picked.

If Peter Piper picked a peck of pickled peppers,

> *Where's the peck of pickled peppers that
> Peter Piper picked?*

—John Harris (1756–1846)

Exercise Title: Enunciation

Exercise Purpose: To strengthen enunciation

Instructions:

Focus on the different ways your mouth moves in order to create different sounds. Repeat the sounds as quickly as you can.

Wewa pronounced wee-wah

A-E-I-O-U (pronounced as long vowels)

Pah Dah Kah Dah

Me Tee Lee See

Make a *Brrrrr* sound by blowing out with your lips closed. It sounds like a motor boat.

Exercise Title:	Mirror
Exercise Purpose:	To focus on body language and create connection

Instructions:

Working with a partner, decide who is A and who is B. Determine who will lead first. For example, if A will be the mover and B will be the Mirror, then B's job is to stay perfectly relaxed and only replicate exactly what A is doing as a mirror image. In other words, if A raises his right hand, B would be raising his left hand.

After a few minutes, stop and relax by shaking out arms and legs. Then switch and have B take over leading the movements.

Start with slow and predictable movements; the main objective is that should someone observe not knowing who is A or B, they would have no idea who is leading and who is following .

After a few minutes keep moving but see if the moves can come from a natural place with neither A nor B leading it.

Exercise Title: What Changed?

Exercise Purpose: To become aware and
understand how much we
observe surroundings and the
people with whom we interact

Instructions:

This is best completed with a partner. Begin by doing
the mirror exercise. Next, stand back to back and taking
turns, ask each other to recall specific details about
things you are each wearing, style of hair, jewelry, etc.
Once you have both recalled as much as possible, turn
and face each other.

Discuss your responses to the following questions:

- How did I do?
- Why do we notice the things we do?
- How do we decide what to pay attention to?
- How can you improve what you observe?
- How does it make me feel when others notice
  me?

Solo:

Observe the details of a room. Close your eyes. Recall
with as much detail as possible what you remember.
Open your eyes. How did you do? Journal the responses
to the questions above.

Exercise Title:	Body Language
Exercise Purpose:	To become aware of body language and how it can affect communication and relationships

Instructions:

Become aware of how you hold your body in the following circumstances:

- Listening to someone
- Speaking with one person
- Speaking to a small group of friends
- Giving a presentation to a small professional group
- Giving a presentation to a larger group of mostly strangers
- Giving directions to someone
- Having an argument
- Speaking when emotional
- Speaking when nervous
- Speaking when confident

What did you notice? Where were your hands? Arms? Were your arms folded against your chest or was your hand covering your mouth? Were you holding something in your hands? If so, what were you doing with the object you were holding? Were your hands gesturing wildly throughout?

So where should you put your hands? For the moment just let them hang loosely at your sides (this is a default position – this is not where your hands will stay). Allow your hands to accentuate what you say without being distracting.

Exercise Title: Does the Story Serve You? Part 1

Exercise Purpose: To build confidence and become
                        aware of stories we create that
                        don't serve us

Instructions:

Read the following scenario:

*You are waiting in an office to see someone (perhaps a client, a
potential client, a boss). The assistant asks you to take a seat.
You do so.*

*You are sitting and watching the assistant. The assistant looks at
you and doesn't smile. Then he/she types something on their
keyboard and then looks at you again. Next the assistant gets up
and walks in the back and then returns a minute later and sits
back down. He/she seems to look at you again. Then he/she
sighs. Then he/she crosses one of his/her legs and lowers his/her
neck as if to stretch it. Finally, he/she sits straight up in the chair
again and audibly sighs. The phone rings and he/she answers it by
naming the company and asking how he/she can help the person.*

Step one: Write down everything you noticed about the
assistant and the actions he/she took. Do not censor
yourself. What ever comes to mind, write it down. Next,
turn the page and continue on to part 2.[2]

---

[2] Exercise adapted from original by Sue Walden, Founder and
Director of ImprovWorks!, a training and consulting organization
dedicated to building Business & Life Skills through Improvisation.

| **Exercise Title:** | Does the Story Serve You? Part 2 |
| **Exercise Purpose:** | To build confidence and become aware of stories we create that don't serve us |

Instructions:

First, reread the scenario from the previous page.

Step two: In the preceding part, you wrote down everything you noticed about the assistant. What types of things did you write down? Were your observations objective or were they an interpretation of what you saw? In other words, did you create a story? Did it "mean" something when the assistant sighed? Did it "mean" something when he/she looked at you and didn't smile?

Review the scenario again. This time only write down the actions of what you see without adding any interpretation. How is this version different? How does adding story affect us adversely? Notice when this comes up in your life and work. If folding arms is simply folding arms, it no longer becomes a measure of what someone might think of you. What would it be like to stop creating stories that do not serve us? [3]

---

[3] Exercise adapted from original by Sue Walden, Founder and Director of ImprovWorks!, a training and consulting organization dedicated to building Business & Life Skills through Improvisation.

Exercise Title: Voice Mirror

Exercise Purpose: To strengthen listening skills

Instructions:

STEP 1. Turn on a radio talk show or the television. Select one voice and begin whispering the words of the speaker **at the same time** the speaker says them, matching them word for word. (Lips are mirroring the words spoken; not mimicking, repeating or echoing.)

STEP 2. As you become more comfortable practicing this, drop the sound and continue to move your mouth, matching/mirroring the words.

STEP 3. Eventually, move the mirror into your mind, so that your thoughts match word-for-word (without external sound or movement) what the speaker is saying. Practice both with eyes open and eyes closed.

Don't rush through these steps—this type of focused listening is not an easy habit to acquire and will take effort and practice. Until you learn how to do it "silently" (in your head), you may want to continue your practice privately with the radio or television.

After you are comfortable with this new tool, you can use it any time you feel your mind start to chatter or wander. Most people find they only need to "Voice Mirror" for 15 to 30 seconds to tune right back in to the speaker.[4]

---

[4] Exercise by Sue Walden, Founder and Director of ImprovWorks!, a training and consulting organization dedicated to building Business & Life Skills through Improvisation.

Exercise Title: Faster Slower

Exercise Purpose: Spontaneity; Creativity; vocal
                          pacing; vocal variety

Instructions:

Working in pairs, first person spontaneously tells a
personal story. Second person listens and signals first
person to speak in a faster, normal, or slower pace by
either showing a thumbs up, a level hand or a thumbs
down throughout the story. Gradually increase the rate
of speed that the signals are given to stretch the story
teller in adapting to various pacing.

Thumbs up = really fast talking
Level hand = normal speed
Thumbs down = slow motion speaking

Repeat by switching roles.

Solo:

Set a timer to beep every 10 seconds and each time it
does, change the pace of the story to be faster. Set a
second timer with a different tone to represent the signal
to go slower.

Exercise Title: Best Worst

Exercise Purpose: Spontaneity; Creativity; Vocal Variety; Flexibility

Instructions:

Working in pairs, first person spontaneously tells a story about an experience he/she had (can be real or imaginary). The person begins the story in a positive way focusing only on wonderful events and circumstances. The second person listens and signals the first person to change the direction of the story by either ringing a bell or showing a thumbs up or a thumbs down throughout the story. When the bell or signal is given, the story teller must now focus on only negative things happening in the story. The next time the signal is given, it reverts back to positive. Each time the switch is made, the story teller needs to justify the transition. Gradually increase the rate of speed that the signals are given to stretch the story teller in adapting more quickly.

Thumbs up = Best

Thumbs down = Worst

This is a wonderful opportunity to practice changing the tone of your voice as you move from positive to negative occurrences in the story. What are some ways you can manipulate your voice to have greater impact? Record yourself telling the story and then play back noting some specific ways you could improve your speaking variety throughout.

Solo:

Set a timer to beep every 10 seconds and each time it does, change the story to be either best or worst. Or, do this as a writing activity switching from best to worst case scenario every few sentences.

Exercise Title: Character Voices

Exercise Purpose: To strengthen vocal variety

Instructions:

There are several ways to improve your ability to bring stories or presentations to life. One of the best ways is to build your repertoire of character voices. The ability to create a voice that depicts the essence of the character that is being spoken about will captivate audiences!

Start by reading a children's book that has many characters. Books by Roald Dahl and J.K. Rowling have a wealth of characters to play with. Each time a new character is introduced, not only change your voice as you read it, but doing something different physically will support maintaining the character voice throughout. Additionally, if you can tap into the emotion of the character, even better!

A character's voice starts in the imagination. Visualize the character and imagine the type of voice he or she might have. If I am playing the part of the Big Friendly Giant in Roald Dahl's The BFG, I imagine him to be very friendly sounding but also somewhat goofy (clumsy, ditsy, nerdy). In order to get that sound, I speak through my nose (as if it is stuffed up) and also from the back and top of my mouth with my tongue placed further back than normal. I will play with this voice until it feels like the best fit.

Set a timer and see how many different voices you can create in 60 seconds based solely on your imagination.

Next, tell a personal story that involves 2 or more characters and each time a character speaks or is referred to, change your voice to match that personality.

Exercise Title: Super Man/Woman Poses

Exercise Purpose: To Experience Being Bold and Increase Confidence

Instructions:

Stand straight with your legs apart and hands on your hips for 2 minutes every day. Or, stand straight with your legs apart and hands straight over your head in a V for 2 minutes. Doing this facing a mirror, even better!

This is a great exercise to do to build confidence in preparation for giving a presentation. Keep a record of how often you do the pose and the results. How did you feel before doing the pose versus afterwards?[5]

---

[5]

This exercise is inspired by Harvard Business School professor Amy Cuddy.

Leadership Presence Exercises

Exercises in this Section:

1. Naming/Misnaming Objects
2. Bang
3. Clap Snap Stomp
4. I Am a Tree
5. What Are You Doing?
6. Magic Present
7. Alphabet Games
8. Last Word, First Word
9. New Choice
10. Silly Questions
11. It's Tuesday
12. Walk Stop

"Leadership is much more an art, a belief, a condition of the heart, than a set of things to do. The visible signs of artful leadership are expressed, ultimately, in its practice."

—Max Depree

Exercise Title: Naming/Misnaming Objects

Exercise Purpose: Joy of Failure; Creativity; Spontaneity

Instructions:

Set a timer for 1 minute. Walk around your environment and name aloud every object you see during that time. If you see a clock, name it "clock." If you see a painting on the wall that has bluish tones, name it "blue painting." In other words, give it the most obvious name, and name as quickly as possible.

Next, set the timer again for 1 minute. This time, walk around your environment and misname aloud everything you see. Say the first thing that comes to mind after you see the object.

If you are able to do this with a partner, have the person record how many things you name during each section of the activity. Repeat this exercise everyday to get faster during the misnaming portion of the exercise.

It is likely that during the misnaming part of this exercise you may experience what we improvisers call a "brain freeze." When this happens, it is as if there are no thoughts or ideas available. This is great! Notice how you feel in this moment. Does it cause stress or anxiety? When do you experience this in other parts of your life? What if you could experience the "joy of failure" instead of panicking? Practice this activity until you are able to easily misname objects fairly rapidly and experience the "joy of failure!"

Exercise Title: Bang

Exercise Purpose: Joy of Failure; Connecting with Others, Being Silly!

Instructions:

There are five hand positions in this game.

Neutral: Forearms parallel to floor at solar plexus level, closed fists and thumbs down on top

Up Center Position: closed fists with thumbs up and move arms up to center above neutral

Up Right: closed fists with thumbs up and move arms up to the right

Up Left: closed fists with thumbs up and move arms up to the left

Down Center Position: closed fists turned down with thumbs out facing down and move straight down center

Always return to the neutral position before moving to the next position. Synchronize with your partner so that you are always arriving at neutral together.

You and partner start at Neutral and then move in different directions without planning, again always returning to neutral and going in sync but as fast as possible. If you and your partner end up in the same position (to the same mirror side), return to neutral and then make "guns" with your hands/thumbs pointing at partner and say "bang" returning to neutral again and continuing the game.

Exercise Title: Clap Snap Stomp

Exercise Purpose: Joy of Failure; Connecting with
                        Others, Being Silly!

Instructions:

Face your partner. Count up to three as fast as you can
taking turns saying each number.

Person 1: One	Person 2: Two	Person 1: Three
Person 2: One	Person 1: Two	Person 2: Three

Play for a while this way alternating as quickly as
possible.

After several rounds replace "one" with a clap.

Person 1: Clap	Person 2: Two	Person 1: Three
Person 2: Clap	Person 1: Two	Person 2: Three

Play for a while this way alternating as quickly as
possible.
After several rounds replace "two" with a two handed
snap.

Person 1: Clap	Person 2: Snap	Person 1: Three
Person 2: Clap	Person 1: Snap	Person 2: Three

Play for a while this way alternating as quickly as
possible.
After several rounds replace "three" with a one foot
stomp.

Person 1: Clap	Person 2: Snap	Person 1: Stomp
Person 2: Clap	Person 1: Snap	Person 2: Stomp

Now, return to first round with only saying numbers.
Is it easier?

Exercise Title:	I Am a Tree
Exercise Purpose:	Accepting and building on offers; Adding the next obvious part of the story

Instructions:

One person says "I am a tree" taking a position as a tree, a second person adds to the picture they are painting, and a third person finishes it. Then the person who was first picks one of the two and leaves the stage, leaving the leftover person on stage as the start of a new picture.

Example:
Person 1: I am a tree
Person 2: I am a leaf on the tree
Person 3: I am the grass under the tree
Person 1: I'll take the grass
1 and 3 leave
Person 2: I am a leaf (restates what they were)
Person 3: I am a salad bowl (they've changed the definition of leaf which is okay)
Person 1: I am salad dressing (supporting creating this new picture)
Etc …

How far from a tree did you end up? What stories could be created from the tableaus created?

Solo:

Playing solo can be really fun! Keep building on each idea and see where you end up.

Exercise Title: What Are You Doing?

Exercise Purpose: Joy of Failure; Creativity;
                        Spontaneity

Instructions:

Person One performs an action such as pantomiming digging a hole. Person Two asks, "What are you doing?" Person One responds by saying something completely different than what he/she are actually doing. Person Two now pantomimes that action. Person One asks, "What are you doing?" Person Two responds by saying something completely different than what he/she is actually doing. Repeat and go as fast as possible.

Solo:

Perform an action and ask yourself, "What am I doing?" Respond with something else. Now do that action and ask yourself again and so on.

Exercise Title: Magic Present

Exercise Purpose: Joy of Failure; Creativity;
Spontaneity; Thinking Outside
the Box

Instructions:

Imagine a conveyor belt filled with gifts and each one is for you! The belt starts moving slowly and your partner hands you the first gift. With each gift you receive, you say, "Thank you" and then name what it is. Be specific. The conveyor belt begins to move faster causing the gifts to be handed to you faster. I recommend setting a timer and playing until the time is up. Start with 2-3 minutes. See how fast you can receive the gifts while still saying thank you and saying what it is.

What did you receive? Were you surprised by any of the gifts you chose? Did you receive anything you didn't like? If so; why do you think you chose a gift you wouldn't enjoy?

Another way of playing is to alternate the giving of gifts back and forth.

Solo:

Play the exact same way except you are removing the imaginary gift from the conveyor belt and naming it as soon as it is in your hands.

Exercise Title: Alphabet Games

Exercise Purpose: Joy of Failure; Creativity; Spontaneity

Instructions:

Alphabet Categories:
With a partner, alternate naming items in a subject area from A to Z.

Example: Names of Women
- A- Alison
- B- Barbara
- C- Catherine
- D- Danielle
- E- Elizabeth, etc.

Alphabet Scenes:
Pick a situation from which to start a scene. Use brief sentences.

Person 1: **A**ll right Doctor, I have the results.
Person 2: **B**ig results I hope?
Person 1: **C**an't fool you. Big they are!
Person 2: **D**im the lights so I can see the x-rays.
Person 1: **E**xactly what I was going to do, etc.

If you get to a letter and can't think of something, make it up. Go as fast as you can!

Solo:

Come up with a category and speaking as fast as possible name an item for each letter consecutively.

Write a scene or paragraph where the next sentence starts with the next letter of the alphabet.

Exercise Title: Last Word, First Word

Exercise Purpose: Joy of Failure; Listening; Dare to be Obvious; Being present; Spontaneity

Instructions:

Pick a situation from which to start a story using brief sentences. The first person starts the story. The next person starts their sentence with the last word that the first person used.

Example:
Person 1: I have your dry **cleaning**.
Person 2: **Cleaning** gives you great **satisfaction**.
Person 1: **Satisfaction** and **joy**.
Person 2: **Joy** helps get the clothes even **cleaner**.
Person 1: **Cleaner** is our motto....   And so on...

Go as fast as you can!

Solo:

Do this as either an oral or written exercise going as fast as you can.

Exercise Title: New Choice

Exercise Purpose: Joy of Failure; Spontaneity; Flexibility

Instructions:

First person tells a story. Second person is the director. Every time the director calls "new choice" the story teller needs to change the last thing he/she said. The director should challenge the story teller by saying, "new choice" in rapid succession until the story teller says something that feels like the best fit. When the "New Choice" prompt has been given, the story teller needs to respond as quickly as possible.

Example:

Story Teller: Once upon a time there was a duck named Freddy.

Director: New choice

Story Teller: named Sam. Everyday Sam would waddle into town to get some ice-cream.

Director: New choice

Story Teller: to get a job. Sam had been unemployed for some time and each day he'd go to the Duck Unemployment Office.

Director: New Choice

Story Teller: He'd go to the farm.

Director: New Choice

Story Teller: He'd go to a party.

And so on…

Solo:

Play with a timer. Set a timer and each time it rings, change the last thing you said.

Exercise Title: Silly Questions

Exercise Purpose: Joy of Failure; Spontaneity; Persuasion; Accepting Offers

Instructions:

The internet is filled with lists of silly questions. Compile a list of questions and then write each one on a slip of paper. Put them in a hat and draw one out. Set a timer for 1 minute and answer the question speaking for the entire time. Focus on speaking as fast as you can.

Play with different ways of responding. Here are a few examples:

1. As an expert of the subject

2. As a sales person selling the idea

3. As a politician or someone in a debate

4. As a slow talking Cowboy in a Western

Exercise Title:	It's Tuesday
Exercise Purpose:	Spontaneity; Persuasion; Accepting Offers, Moving Story Forward; Playing Big

Instructions:

First person says a very simple and non emotional or impactful statement.

Examples:

- It's Tuesday
- Here is your coffee.
- I have your umbrella.
- The milk is in the fridge.
- The cat needs to be fed.

The second person responds to the statement with a HUGE and over the top reaction justifying the reaction with the words being said. The purpose of the exercise is not about doing a scene but giving opportunity for having large emotional reactions. Notice how often the reaction chosen is positive versus negative. If leaning toward negative, work on having big positive reactions.

Exercise Title: Walk Stop

Exercise Purpose: Spontaneity; Joy in Failure;
Becoming aware of positive and
negative thought patterns

Instructions:

With a partner, one person directs by giving the order
"walk" or "stop". The other person does as directed.
After a minute, change the meaning of the words to the
opposite. First person gives commands but "walk"
means "stop" and vice versa. The second person
follows commands with new meaning.

After a minute, add the commands, "clap" and "stomp"
to the reversed meaning commands of "walk" "stop".

After a minute, reverse meaning of "clap" "stomp" and
give commands with reverse meaning "walk" "Stop"
commands.

Add in one other set of commands and do the same
with reversing and adding two other reversed
commands.

Moving the Story Forward Exercises

Exercises in this Section:

1. Yes And/Yes But

2. Story Spine

3. Fortunately Unfortunately

4. 60 Second Future Life

5. Observing Mindset

6. Goal Setting

7. Backwards Mapping

8. Time Plan

9. Ideal Time Plan

10. Productivity *Stick to it Sticks*^{TM}

"Because if you take a risk, you just might find what you're looking for."

—Susane Colasanti

Exercise Title:	Yes And/Yes But
Exercise Purpose:	Accepting offers; brainstorming; moving the story forward

Instructions:

Working as a group, the goal is to plan an event. It could be a party, a trip, or even a business meeting. During the first round, every time someone gives their idea, someone else should answer, "Yes, BUT... and give the reason why that is not going to work." This might start to sound strangely familiar, and like many business meetings or planning committees.

During the second round, the response should be "Yes, AND" add something that builds on the first idea". The next person adds something to that continuing to build positively each time.

After the exercise is complete, debrief and discuss how the terms affected the group energy and also the kinds of ideas that resulted from each round.

Solo:

Write down the first idea and then writing the words, "yes but" negate each offer until you are tired of doing the exercise. Repeat and this time build on each idea by adding to it positively with a "Yes and." If it gets absurd, that's okay. Notice how you feel during each phase of the exercise and then review the results. There may be nuggets from both rounds! Use Yes And to create presentation or speech topics.

Exercise Title: Story Spine

Exercise Purpose: Spontaneity; Persuasion; Accepting Offers, Moving Story Forward; Playing Big

Instructions:

Once upon a time…

Everyday…(can repeat)

Until one day…

Because of that (can repeat)

Until finally….

And ever since then…

Use the spine to tell the story of your business, your life as it is now and then how you'd like it to be. Here is an example of the spine applied to my business journey:

> **Once upon a time** there was a woman named Lisa who was a teacher. **Everyday** she taught children how to be better communicators. **Everyday** she wished she could have a job that was more creative. **Everyday** (even though the kids were great) she wished she could work with adults. **Until one day** she went on vacation to Thailand. **Because of that** she ended up surviving the SE Asia tsunami. **Because of that** she made huge life changes. **Because of that** she moved overseas. **Because of that** she developed a connection between improvisation and communication. **Until finally** she launched Improv Consultants and began working with adults in a creative way.

Exercise Title:	Story Spine (continued)
Exercise Purpose:	Spontaneity; Persuasion; Accepting Offers, Moving Story Forward; Playing Big

Instructions:

And ever since then Improv Consultants has been supporting businesses, schools, and individuals in creating something dynamic out of being spontaneous!

Story Spine is also an effective speech writing tool. Use it to build the speech and then once the draft is written— review, edit, and revise to support writing the final copy.[6]

---

[6] Story Spine was created by Kenn Adams, the Artistic Director of the San Francisco Bay Area's Synergy Theater and the author of the book How to Improvise a Full Length Play, The Art of Spontaneous Theater. www.SynergyTheater.com"

Exercise Title: Fortunately, Unfortunately

Exercise Purpose: Spontaneity; Finding Positive Solutions; Thinking Outside the Box

Instructions:

This is an example of how it would be played with two people doing a imaginary scene.

First person says something like, *"Fortunately, I have the day off today."*

Second person responds by saying, *"Unfortunately, you have a lot of work to catch up on."*

First person says, *"Fortunately, I hired an assistant and the work is all taken care of."*

Second person, *"Unfortunately, it's raining out so you're stuck inside on your day off."*

First person, *"Fortunately, I have a wonderful book to read as I cozy up on the couch."*

Second person, *"Unfortunately, the dog ate your book."*

First person, *"Fortunately, I'm sleepy and taking a nap sounds even better!"*

Second person, *"Unfortunately, the sound of construction next door prevents you from sleeping."*

First person, *"Fortunately, it's the sound of my new home being built which makes me excited and not needing to sleep anymore!"*

And so forth...

Exercise Title: Fortunately, Unfortunately
                          (continued)

Exercise Purpose: Spontaneity; Finding Positive
                          Solutions; Thinking Outside the Box

Instructions:

Solo

Do this as a written exercise about something real and current in your life. A wonderful variation is to start with *unfortunately* and end up with *fortunately*.

"Unfortunately, I've lost my voice before a presentation. Fortunately, I am very expressive and will use a combination of video, music, and power point to convey my message...etc."

Exercise Title: 60 Second Future Life

Exercise Purpose: To gain clarity to support setting goals

Instructions:

Imagine it is 10 years from now. Perform the activity as explained in 60 Second Life and this time relate all that's happened in the past future and imaginary 10 years.

Then the listening partner retells what they heard. The "telling" partner only listens to what was heard without commenting, correcting, or interjecting. Then the process is reversed. After both partners have completed the cycle, debrief the process by asking yourselves the following questions:

- How did that feel?
- What actually happened as we did that?
- What did you learn?
- Were you surprised by what you created?
- Would you like to redo it and have different outcomes?
- What would it take to accomplish all that you created?

This activity can be replayed with different time increments. Try doing it with only 1 year in the future or similarly 25 years in the future.

Solo:

Set a timer for 1 minute. Write about your life for 1 minute as fast as you can- stream of consciousness. Upon completing the exercise, respond to the debrief questions above by writing down your responses.

Exercise Title: Observing Mindset

Exercise Purpose: Moving Story Forward; Perception; Positivity

Instructions:

Throughout the week observe your mindset and the stories you create. (Review the activity, "Does the Story Serve You?").

Humans tend to tell stories where the scared alone teenager ends up in the dangerously dark basement. What represents the dark basement that you go into? Make note of the following:

- What was the story?

- What was the situation?

- What could be a new focus or way of looking at the situation?

Without judgment, observe the stories you create and ask yourself the following questions:

- What do I get out of creating a story with this outcome?

- What would the story look like if I created a positive outcome?

- How might I respond differently if I didn't create a story at all?

- If I employ voice mirroring, does it change the pace or tone of the stories I create? Does it slow it down? Does it stop the story creating all together?

We have the choice to change our mindset at any point. If you become aware that you are creating a story that ultimately does not serve the situation, focus on active listening instead.

Exercise Title: Goal Setting

Exercise Purpose: Accepting Offers, Moving Story Forward; Playing Big

Instructions:

Goals are an important part of moving the story forward. Goals need to be SMART.[7]

Specific
Measurable
Attainable
Realistic
Timely

Specific Goals have a much better chance of being accomplished than a general or vague goal. Ask yourself the following questions:

- Who is involved?

- What do I want to accomplish?

- Where is the location?

- When do I want to have this done by and is there a timeline needed?

- Which requirements and constraints are needed?

- Why is this goal important?

EXAMPLE: I will publish a handbook for business professionals that supports building executive presence using improvisation.

---

[7] The first known use of the term [SMART Goals] occurs in the November 1981 issue of *Management Review* by George T. Doran.

Meyer, Paul J (2003). "What would you do if you knew you couldn't fail? Creating S.M.A.R.T. Goals: *Attitude Is Everything: If You Want to Succeed Above and Beyond*. Meyer Resource Group, Incorporated, The. ISBN 978-0-89811-304-4.

Exercise Title:	Goal Setting (continued)
Exercise Purpose:	Accepting Offers, Moving Story Forward; Playing Big

Instructions:

Measurable Goals establish a criteria for measuring progress and success which helps to keep on track. To determine if the goal is measurable, ask questions such as:

- How much? How many?
- How will I know when it is accomplished?

EXAMPLE: I will work on my book every week. Or...I will complete one section per week. It will be accomplished when all four sections are done as with the intro and pages in the back.

Goals that are important to you have a better chance of being **Attainable.** Being passionate about your goal leads to developing the attitudes, abilities, skills, and financial capacity to reach them.

EXAMPLE: I am very passionate about the work I do and seeing my clients get results is truly motivating!

Exercise Title:	Goal Setting (continued)
Exercise Purpose:	Accepting Offers, Moving Story Forward; Playing Big

Instructions:

Is the goal **Realistic?** Are you willing and able to work toward it? A high goal may be more motivating than a low goal. This is a personal choice. What will motivate you to complete all the necessary steps to reach the goal?

EXAMPLE: The book will be mostly comprised of exercises with some narrative. The book will be between 90-100 pages. This is realistic and attainable.

A goal needs to be **timely**. When do you need/want to have it completed by?

EXAMPLE: Setting a deadline of July 15th will ensure that this book is complete and ready for publication for upcoming speaking dates that I have in August and September. I have consistent time during the summer to work and complete this book.

Exercise Title: Backwards Mapping

Exercise Purpose: Moving Story Forward

Instructions:

Backwards mapping was something that I found quite useful when teaching. The idea is to start at the culminating activity or the end point of the goal and work backwards in order to effectively plan and reach your goal.

Once you have identified your SMART goals, you will use this strategy to work backwards to determine what you need to do in order to accomplish your goal.

Starting with the end result of your goal, ask yourself, what do you need to know or do in order to reach that goal? Here is an example of the backwards mapping process when applied to the publishing of this book:

1. Upload my completed text to the publishing site
2. Review the completed proof read copy by my editor
3. Submit my draft to my editor
4. Find and hire an editor
5. Click save on my final draft
6. Review the entire book once complete
7. Write out the instructions for completing each exercise
8. Write an introduction, table of contents, and include other specific tools/resources that will support making this a valuable resource
9. Review my session notes and planners to determine the best exercises for inclusion in the book
10. Determine the layout/size for the book
11. Create an outline for the book
12. Set aside time during the week to write the book

Exercise Title: Time Plan

Exercise Purpose: Moving Story Forward

Instructions:

The first step in creating an ideal time plan is to observe and note what you are currently spending your time on. For one week, keep a journal of where your time goes. See if you can account for every minute of each day.

At the end of the week, review how you spent your time and create categories that you will use to create an ideal time plan.

Categories might include:

- Travel time (driving or walking from one location to another)
- Friends/Family
- Dating
- Work
- Work maintenance (things like catching up on emails, paying bills, etc)
- Exercise
- Health
- Sleeping
- Eating
- Preparing meals

Do you notice any patterns? Are you satisfied with how you spent your time? Are there categories that were lacking or not addressed at all? What could you do to shift your schedule to fit those things in? Create a time plan for the upcoming week with an emphasis on including things that are important to you.

Exercise Title: Ideal Time Plan

Exercise Purpose: Moving Story Forward; Playing Big;
Living Your Dream

Instructions:

Once you have a sense how you are presently spending your time, map out how you'd like to spend your time in your ideal world. The sky is the limit. What would you like to put first? Your brain will rationalize and want to find excuses for why this won't work. Refer back to YES AND…and allow yourself to plan freely. This is just an exercise. No need to commit to the plan you create but why not create one that makes you truly happy? Create a plan that is in alignment with your values.

When I did this exercise, I learned that I was spending a lot of time on work and hardly any time on self-care or with friends. No wonder I was overwhelmed and slightly stressed. Upon creating a new plan, I made sure to add space for time with friends and time for me! Shortly after creating this new time plan I met a wonderful man whom I spent time with for the next year! Making space in my weekly plan for time with friends, family, and me made a huge difference in my overall morale. Try it! It's a joy to create a vision of how you want to spend your time.

Exercise Title: Productivity *Stick to it Sticks*[TM]

Exercise Purpose: Moving Story Forward

Instructions:

What are the things in your life or business that no matter how many times they end up on your 'to do' list, they just don't seem to get done? Perhaps it is stretching, or taking some time to journal, or cold calling. Make a list of those items and then write one on each popsicle stick. Place the sticks in a container marked "Action Items." On a new set of popsicle sticks, write lengths of times on each one. I usually recommend not exceeding 30 minutes.

Supply List
• Popsicle Sticks
• Permanent Markers
• 2 Containers
• Timer

5 Minutes

10 Minutes

15 Minutes

20 Minutes

30 Minutes

Place these sticks face down (so that you can't see the time) in a separate container marked "Time."

You are ready. Once or more a day, pull a stick from each container. One will be your action item and the other will tell you how long you get to do it for. Notice I used the word "get" instead of "have." The more we can change our mindset to support the idea that we get to do these tasks, the easier it will be to achieve them.

Once you have pulled an action item and a time stick, set a timer for the designated time and then enjoy getting to do that task for a short and finite amount of time.

"Even if you fall on your face, you are still moving forward."

—Victor Kiam

Sample Improv Menu

- What were some successes over the past week?
- What were some challenges over the past week?
- What would you like to work on today?

Internal Presence Exercises

1. Vertebrae Roll Up and Down
2. Breathing
3. Counting 1-8
4. Who Are You?

Professional Presence Exercises

1. Enunciation
2. Does the Story Serve You?
3. Voice Mirror
4. Super Man/Woman Poses

Leadership Presence Exercises

1. What are you doing?
2. I am a Tree
3. New Choice

Moving the Story Forward

1. Yes And Yes But
2. Story Spine
3. Time Plan

Activity Index

Exercise	*Page #*
60 Second Future Life	54
60 Second Life	15
Alphabet Games	42
Bang	37
Best Worst	32
Body Language	27
Breathing	10
Breathing and Vocalizing	11
Character Voices	33
Clap Snap Stomp	38
Counting 1-8	12
Does the Story Serve You? Part 1	28
Does the Story Serve You? Part 2	29
Enunciation	24
Faster Slower	31
Fortunately Unfortunately	52-53
Goal Setting	56-58
I Am a Tree	39
Ideal Day	18
It's Tuesday	46
Last Word, First Word	43
Magic Present	41

Mirror   25

Naming/Misnaming Objects   36

New Choice   44

Observing Mindset   55

Pros and Cons   19

Silly Questions   45

Story Spine   50-51

Super Man/Woman Poses   34

Tongue Twisters   23

Vertebrae Roll Up and Down   9

Vision Board   20

Visualization   16

Vocal Tones   22

Voice Mirror   30

Walk Stop   47

What Are You Doing?   40

What Changed?   26

What Do You See?   17

Who Am I?   14

Who Are You?   13

Yes And/Yes But   49

About The Author

Lisa Safran, MA, owner of Improv Consultants facilitates professional and staff development workshops around the world to demonstrate how to use improvisation to build strong leadership, communication skills, and strengthen teamwork. Lisa has provided services to a broad range of businesses ranging from tech firms to realtors. She helps business owners, managers, and executives to develop comfort and ease while leading effective and engaging presentations.

In addition to <u>Executive Presence Improv Style,</u> Safran published <u>Reading and Writing Come Alive: Using Improvisation to Build Literacy</u> a book for educators.

ImprovConsultants
Strategy, Innovation, Results

To learn more about coaching or training programs, please visit http://www.improvconsultants.com or contact Lisa Safran directly at info@improvconsultants.com.

Made in the USA
San Bernardino, CA
16 September 2017